What Are Faces For?

Story by Adria F. Klein and Jack Winder
Illustrations by Bob Reese

Dominie Press, Inc.

What are faces for?

You will find many things
on your face.

Two eyes for looking.

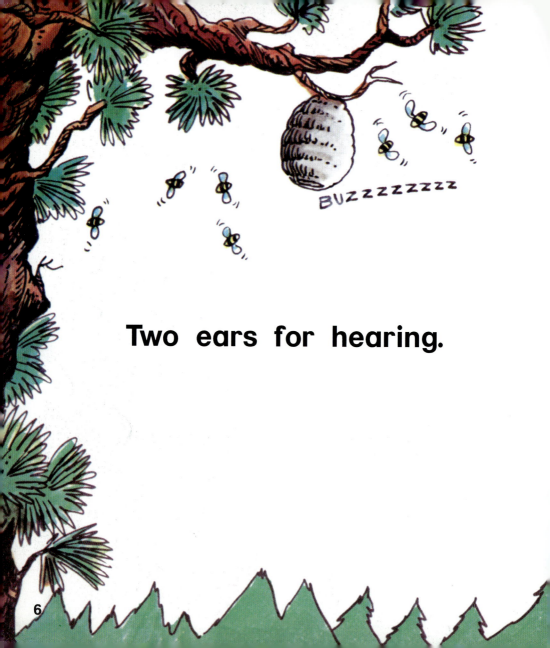

BUZzzzzzzz

Two ears for hearing.

Buzz!

One nose for smelling.

Phew!

Two lips for talking.

Lots of teeth
for chewing our food.

One tongue for touching
where my tooth was.

15

One mouth
for blowing up a balloon.

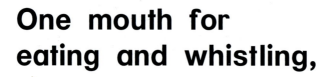

**One mouth for
eating and whistling,**

but not while
eating a cracker.

What are faces for?

They are for looking, hearing, smelling, talking, chewing, eating, and lots of other things!

I am a Fifty-Word Book

My fifty words are:

a	not
and	of
are	on
balloon	One
blowing	other
but	our
Buzz	Phew
chewing	smelling
cracker	talking
ears	teeth
eating	things
eyes	tongue
face (faces)	tooth
find	touching
food	They
for	Two
Growl	up
hearing	was
lips	What
looking	where
lots	while
many	whistling
mouth	will
my	You
nose	your

Published by:

🐚 **Dominie Press, Inc.**

1949 Kellogg Avenue
Carlsbad, California 92008 USA

www.dominie.com
ISBN 0-7685-2259-5
Printed in Singapore by PH Productions Pte Ltd
1 2 3 4 5 PH 07 06 05